Pavel Vasilyev

# Modernity, Capitalism and the Pathologies of Jewish Health: Anti-Semitic Elements of Fin-De-Siècle Medical Discourse

GRIN Publishing

**Bibliographic information published by the German National Library:**

The German National Library lists this publication in the National Bibliography; detailed bibliographic data are available on the Internet at http://dnb.dnb.de .

**Imprint:**

Copyright © 2010 GRIN Verlag, Open Publishing GmbH
Print and binding: Books on Demand GmbH, Norderstedt Germany
ISBN: 978-3-640-78333-5

**This book at GRIN:**

http://www.grin.com/en/e-book/163782/modernity-capitalism-and-the-pathologies-of-jewish-health-anti-semitic

**GRIN - Your knowledge has value**

Since its foundation in 1998, GRIN has specialized in publishing academic texts by students, college teachers and other academics as e-book and printed book. The website www.grin.com is an ideal platform for presenting term papers, final papers, scientific essays, dissertations and specialist books.

**Visit us on the internet:**

http://www.grin.com/

http://www.facebook.com/grincom

http://www.twitter.com/grin_com

# MODERNITY, CAPITALISM AND THE PATHOLOGIES OF JEWISH HEALTH: ANTI-SEMITIC ELEMENTS OF FIN-DE-SIÈCLE MEDICAL DISCOURSE

(Pavel Vasilyev)

While we are generally eager to recognize the importance of medicine and medical discourse in the contemporary world, it is not always easy to connect the history of medicine with the study of anti-Semitism. Indeed, this topic has received relatively little attention from scholars. However, I will argue that a closer look at the anti-Semitic elements of medical discourse is an important and promising enterprise. If we examine the most notorious manifestation of modern anti-Semitism, the Shoah, we can easily see that it was at least partially prepared and justified by the authority of medical science.[1] In contemporary post-modern world, academics and laymen alike often question the objectivity of science and its ability to coherently explain the world[2], but for the late 19th and early 20th century Europeans Science was perhaps the highest authority and the main reference point. Accordingly, when the genocide of the Jews was justified scientifically, it became much more difficult to resist it. In a certain way, medical science gave to modern anti-Semitism the same degree of legitimacy as Christian religion delegated to medieval anti-Judaism centuries earlier.

The focus of this paper is on the same region where the Nazi genocide was planned and carried out (Central Europe) and on the German-language medical discourse (German being arguably the most important language for European scientific discourse for a long period). However, I will concentrate on the period that preceded the Nazi rule (late 19th and early 20th centuries) – and for some reasons. As scholars struggle to comprehend the horrific design of the Holocaust, they come to the understanding that it is impossible to explain the Nazi genocide without looking at the rise and developments of modern anti-Semitism in Wilhelmine Germany (even though it is absolutely necessary to differentiate between the two). This approach was implemented by Shulamit Volkov in her attempt to distinguish "the written matter" and

---

[1]     Henry Friedlander, *The Origins of Nazi Genocide: From Euthanasia to the Final Solution* (Chapel Hill: University of North Carolina Press, 1995).
[2]     See., e.g., Georges Canguilhem, *On the Normal and the Pathological* (Dordrecht, Holland: Reidel, 1978*)*; Karin Knorr-Cetina, *Die Fabrikation von Erkentniss: Zur Anthropologie der Naturwissenschaft* (Frankfurt am Main: Suhrkamp, 1984); Bruno Latour and Steve Woolgar, *Laboratory Life: The Construction of Scientific Facts* (Princeton: Princeton University Press, 1986).

"the spoken word"[3] as well as by some medical history scholars dealing with continuity/discontinuity debate.[4]

Accordingly, in this paper I will look at fin-de-siècle German-language medical discourse to locate and analyze anti-Semitic sentiments and critique of Jewish health that were often inherent in it. In particular, I am interested why (and how) various alleged pathologies of Jewish health were associated with modernity and capitalist economy. Additionally, I want to trace the influence that fin-de-siècle medical anti-Semitism had in the later period. In doing so, I plan to rely largely on such medical history classics as Sander Gilman's "The Jew's Body" and John Efron's "Medicine and the German Jews" - as well as the number of works by Klaus Hödl and Daniel Wildmann.

**Scientification of Stereotypes: The Nature and Content of Anti-Semitic Medical Discourse**

As soon as we approach turn-of-the-century medical discourse and label it anti-Semitic, we must face an important challenge. There is a seeming contradiction between flourishing anti-Jewish sentiments among the doctors and the statistically proven over-representation of the Jews in the medical profession in the region.[5] Yet most of these Jewish doctors were reluctant to challenge the dominant discourse that presented the Jewish people as fundamentally diseased and pathological. To better understand and explain this seeming contradiction, we should discuss the nature, content and the lines of reasoning of fin-de-siècle medical anti-Semitism in more detail.

As Klaus Hödl has successfully demonstrated, late 19th and early 20th century medical theory was "highly influenced by extant, racially determined conceptions", "amenable to biased views of ethnic groups" and "its findings reflected ... widely shared prejudices"[6]. However, the language of medicine of that time was becoming increasingly scientific and sophisticated. Hödl explains this by arguing that late 19th century medical anti-Semitism was in fact occupied mostly with "scientification" of the

---

[3] Shulamit Volkov, "The Written Matter and the Spoken Word: On the Gap Between Pre-1914 and Nazi Anti-Semitism," in *Unanswered Questions: Nazi Germany and the Genocide of the Jews*, ed. François Furet (New York: Schocken Books, 1989), 33-53.

[4] Paul F. Lerner, *Hysterical Men: War, Psychiatry and the Politics of Trauma in Germany, 1890-1930* (Ithaca: Cornell University Press, 2003).

[5] John M. Efron, *Medicine and the German Jews: A History* (New Haven: Yale University Press, 2001), 10.

[6] Klaus Hödl, "The Black Body and the Jewish Body: A Comparison of Medical Images," *Patterns of Prejudice* 36 (2002): 34.

already existing stereotypes, not with the creation of the new ones.[7] This new language of the science might seem modern, but the anti-Semitic physicians were generally repeating the accusations against the Jews that had existed since the Middle Ages – but in a more fashionable way.

To examine this premise, we should have a look at the content of anti-Semitic medical discourse. Indeed, the Jews were associated with many negative features ranging from unpleasant form of nose to undecipherable speech to susceptibility to neuroses.[8] Other critics would note such alleged qualities as the stunted growth of the Jews or the lack of muscular power.[9] Many of these accusations culminated in the proclamations that male Jews were essentially effeminate and unsuitable for military service.[10] It may seem to go in line with the modern narratives of such different persons as Jellinek or Weininger, but in fact the association of the male Jews with women existed for a long time since the Middle Ages. For example, Jewish males have been thought to menstruate since medieval times.[11]

In fact, it would be inaccurate to say that the Jews were only imagined in a negative way. Fin-de-siècle medicine ascribed to the Jews many seemingly positive and useful features – such as inborn intelligence[12] or immunity to tuberculosis related to the perceived Jewish ability to adapt to any circumstances[13]. But even those positive qualities were often seen in a perverted way. For example, the above-mentioned features could be associated with physical weakness or cosmopolitanism (lack of proper national feeling). However good may intelligence and adaptability sound to us, for fin-de-siècle public the feeling of patriotism based on blood and physical strength was a much more plausible character trait.

**The Lines of Reasoning: Anti-Modernism and Anti-Semitism**

The underlying explanation of the various alleged pathologies of Jewish health

---

[7]     Klaus Hödl, "Medizinischer Antisemitismus oder Antisemitismus in der Medizin? Historische Wurzeln und Charakterisierungsversuche eines Phänomens," in *Antisemitismusforschung in den Wissenschaften*, ed. Werner Bergmann and Mona Körte (Berlin: Metropol, 2004), 175.

[8]     Idem, "Der "jüdische Körper" in seiner Differenz. Textuelle und performative Konstruktionen." in *Marginalisierte Körper. Beiträge zur Soziologie und Geschichte des anderen Körpers*, ed. Torsten Junge and Imke Schmincke, (Münster: Unrast, 2007), 69-70.

[9]     Efron, 142.

[10]     Hödl, *Der "jüdischer Körper" in seiner Differenz*, 69-70. See also Efron, 142-150.

[11]     Klaus Hödl, "Der jüdische Körper als Stigma," *Österreichische Zeitschrift für Geschichtswissenschaften* 2 (1997): 212-213 and Idem, *Der "jüdischer Körper" in seiner Differenz*, 69.

[12]     Sander L. Gilman, *The Jew's Body* (New York: Routledge, 1991), 128-149.

[13]     Hödl, *The Black Body*, 22-24.

can probably be summarized in one word – modernity. Fin-de-siècle Europe started to doubt the values of progress and established that modernity mostly brings disease and degeneration. The Jews were often perceived as over-educated urban middle-class group at the forefront of change and modernity. I will show that many accusations that ascribed to the Jews physical and moral degeneration and effeminacy were in fact attacks against capitalism and modernity (the latter two being often seen as the Jewish enterprises).

There were, of course, explanations of pathological Jewish health that were rooted in tradition rather than modernity. Many anti-Semitic physicians view the causes of the specificity of the Jewish health in such elements of Judaism as relative endogamy, ritual prohibitions and kosher food laws.[14] However, here we must recall the peculiar double character of the Jews as being simultaneously modern and backward that has so often been invoked in anti-Semitic thought in various contexts[15].

As we have already mentioned, around turn of the century the benefits of modernity were challenged. But for the 19th -century Europeans modernity was not just an abstract concept - it had many concrete manifestations in the contemporary world. One of these facets was definitely capitalism - and the association of the Jews with capitalism had a very long tradition. In fact, the very word *Jude* in the 19th-century German language was synonymous to huckster (that is to a capitalist with a very pejorative connotation). Many influential thinkers from Marx to Sombart have excessively criticized Jewish involvement in modern capitalism and even presented the capitalism on the whole as a Jewish enterprise – the thesis that has been most recently revisited by Jerry Z. Muller.[16] In medical context, the pathologies of Jewish health could have easily been explained as the result of the excessive Jewish involvement in the capitalist economy.

Another relevant issue is that of cosmopolitanism. The Jews who were the nation scattered across all the continents but with no independent state of their own were obvious deviants in the age of nation-states - but cosmopolitanism was not only a political issue. It was also closely related to transnational patterns of operation inherent in modern capitalism and all the matters that we have already discussed above. In

---

[14]     Efron, 130, 155.

[15]     Paul F. Lerner, "Circulation and Representation: Jews, Department Stores and Cosmopolitan Consumption in Germany, ca. 1880s-1930s," *European Review of History* 17 (2010) (forthcoming): 16; Derek J. Penslar, *Shylock's Children: Economics and Jewish Identity in Modern Europe* (Berkeley: University of California Press, 2001), 5, 11-49.

[16]     Jerry Z. Muller, *Capitalism and the Jews* (Princeton: Princeton University Press, 2010).

relation to medical anti-Semitism, cosmopolitanism comes up in relation to the debate about Jews' extraordinary ability for acclimatization[17] that I have already mentioned.

Finally, there was yet another facet of modernity that negatively influenced Jewish health – that of urbanization. The Jews were indeed an urban group *par excellence*, and they tried to use all the opportunities provided by the cities as soon as they were permitted to do so. But when fin-de-siècle culture brought renewed interest in the traditional and natural, it is not really surprising that the alleged Jewish predisposition for neuroses was explained as the logical result of their choice to live in the modern city with all its stress and uncertainty.[18] In other contexts, the alleged shortness of the Jews was linked to such specific residential and occupational features as urbanization and the predominance of indoor jobs.[19]

Summarizing the debate about the origins of the 'problem', we can note that the Jews' bodies were often seen as extraordinary and pathological precisely because their bearers were so modern. The term *modern* that is used here is to be understood in a broad sense as a shortcut for many diverse and often unrelated manifestations of modernity – including but not limited to cosmopolitanism, liberalism, capitalism, urbanization and education.

Moreover, the association of the Jews with modernity was often an illusion. For example, in Central Europe the Jews were indeed widely present in the professions and businesses, but the majority of them remained poor and traditional, as the examples from fin-de-siècle Vienna convincingly demonstrate[20]. Indeed, the "ideal types" of the late-19th century Viennese Jewry were not all-mighty bankers and financiers but rather "the peddler, the old-clothes dealer, and the *Lumpenproletarier,* scraping an irregular existence on the periphery of the economic system".[21] However, for our purposes it is important that the Jews were seen as modern - and often perceived themselves as such.

### Solutions of the Problem: Possible Responses to Medical Anti-Semitism

We can now come closer to the explanation of the universal reception of medical anti-Semitism – even among the Jews. Even more strikingly, as we have seen, the accusations among the Jews were mostly re-formulated medieval stereotypes that just

---

[17]     Hödl, *The Black Body*, 22-24; Idem, *Medizinischer Antisemitismus*, 172-173.
[18]     Efron, 153.
[19]     Hödl, *The Black Body*, 30.
[20]     Ivar Oxaal and Walter R. Weitzmann. "The Jews of Pre-1914 Vienna: An Exploration of Basic Sociological Dimensions," *Leo Baeck Institute Yearbook* 30 (1985): 419.
[21]     Ibid., 424.

did not correspond to the reality. But there were still some reasons, why anti-Semitic statements inherent in fin-de-siècle medical thought were so widely discussed and so enthusiastically embraced.

The most important reason is the authority of science, which was universally perceived as an objective, trustful and verifiable source of information about the surrounding world. In fact, the adherence to the principles of positivist-type scientific inquiry (however modern it may seem) can be a perceived as an another variant of cultural code that was widely embraced in fin-de-siècle Central Europe.[22] As for other reasons, perhaps, it is important to invoke once again that persistent association of the Jews with modernity was combined with strong anti-Modernist feelings that emerged around turn of the century and traditional Jewish perspectives on history in the diaspora period as regress and degeneration.

However, even when the accusations stated by medical anti-Semites were taken for granted, the problem remained unsolved. In other words, how can one deal with the pathologies of Jewish health? One of the most obvious Jewish responses to the accusations of being weak and ill is, of course, involvement in sports. Jewish sports and gymnastics societies that have flourished in Germany around 1900 clearly demonstrate this trend.[23] Notably, those responses did not challenge anti-Semitic medical perceptions – they just acknowledged that it is through the improvement of socio-economic conditions and physical work that the corporeal strength is restored/improved.[24] Thus, these movements corresponded nicely to the Zionist longing for the Jewish regeneration and the recreation of muscle Jewry (*Muskeljudentum*) that was so famously invoked by Max Nordau[25] (and indeed many of these sports clubs were openly Zionist[26]).

Another set of responses would include involvement in the projects of universal salvation that would promise to radically change the world and transform the society.

---

[22] For the discussion on "cultural codes", see Shulamit Volkov, "Antisemitism as a Cultural Code: Reflections on the History and Historiography of Antisemitism in Imperial Germany," *Leo Baeck Institute Yearbook* 23 (1978): 25-46.

[23] Daniel Wildmann, "Jewish Gymnasts and Their Corporeal Utopias in Imperial Germany," in *Emancipation through Muscles. Jews and Sports in Europe*, ed. Michael Brenner and Gideon Reuveni (Lincoln: University of Nebraska Press, 2006), 27-43. See also Idem, *Der veränderbare Körper. Jüdische Turner, Männlichkeit und das Wiedergewinnen von Geschichte in Deutschland um 1900* (Tübingen: Mohr Siebeck, 2009).

[24] Idem, *Jewish Gymnasts*, 28.

[25] Michael Brenner, "Introduction: Why Jews and Sports," in *Emancipation through Muscles*, 4-5.

[26] Ibid., 1-7.

Indeed, active Jewish involvement in the various universalist movements that emerged around turn of the century (ranging from psychoanalysis to feminism to Esperantism) shows that many Jews felt an urgent need to dramatically transform the political, social, economic and cultural landscape of the world they were living in. Among other things, such transformation would certainly be supposed to have a positive effect on the Jewish health.

One of the most radical forms of such salvation projects would be belligerent anti-capitalism in the form of communism that would seek to destroy the "disease" that was often perceived as the modern incarnation of Judaism – capitalism. The dramatic socio-economic change was supposed to improve the health conditions of the formerly oppressed classes - and in fact many early Soviet thinkers (among them many Jews) were occupied with the projects that would transform and improve the bodies of the workers and build a new Soviet man.[27]

Finally, the ultimate response to the medical anti-Semitism would be Nazism. As Klaus Hödl has put it, "the body is an important factor of identity construction" and the body of the Other appears as the fundamental opposition.[28] And as soon as the source of pathology within the German national body was located in the Jews, it is not very surprising that some people would come up with an idea to eliminate the Jewish presence in Germany – arguing along the lines of the medical discourse that when the part of the human body is so much contaminated it should just be amputated.

Our analysis have found that the Jews occupied a special place in the late 19th and early 20th century German-language medical discourse. In most cases, the Jewish body was associated with pathologies and diseases, and behind the scientific language there were centuries-old medieval stereotypes. Perhaps more importantly, the alleged pathologies of the Jewish health were perceived as the results of Jewish over-involvement in the modernity project and closely linked to capitalism, cosmopolitanism and urbanization. Finally, medical anti-Semitism appears to have served as an inspiration or point of reference for many ideological and political movements that would finally determine the face of 20-th century Europe.

---

[27]     On this topic see, e.g., Stefan Plaggenborg, *Revolutionskultur: Menschenbilder und kulturelle Praxis in Sowjetrussland zwischen Oktoberrevolution und Stalinismus* (Cologne: Böhlau, 1996) and Tricia Starks, *The Body Soviet: Propaganda, Hygiene, and the Revolutionary State* (Madison: University of Wisconsin Press, 2008).
[28]     Hödl, *Der "jüdische Körper" in seiner Differenz*, 63.

In conclusion, I would like to designate some prospects for the further research. In my opinion, it would be very interesting to further analyze and compare the rhetoric and the lines of reasoning that were used by the physicians describing diseases – and by politicians or journalists dealing with the Jews. My hypothesis is that there might have been many similarities between the two cases. Another potential direction of research would be to critically compare the experiences of several countries and the places that the Jews occupied in the medical discourse in different national  contexts (the first successful attempts have already been made by Klaus Hödl[29]).

---

[29]     Idem, *The Black Body.*

# Bibliography

1. Brenner, Michael and Gideon Reuveni, eds. *Emancipation through Muscles. Jews and Sports in Europe.* Lincoln: University of Nebraska Press, 2006.

2. Canguilhem, Georges. *On the Normal and the Pathological.* Dordrecht, Holland: Reidel, 1978.

3. Efron, John M. *Medicine and the German Jews: A History.* New Haven: Yale University Press, 2001.

4. Friedlander, Henry. *The Origins of Nazi Genocide: From Euthanasia to the Final Solution.* Chapel Hill: University of North Carolina Press, 1995.

5. Gilman, Sander L. *The Jew's Body.* New York: Routledge, 1991.

6. Hödl, Klaus. "Der jüdische Körper als Stigma." *Österreichische Zeitschrift für Geschichtswissenschaften* 2 (1997): 212-230.

7. Hödl, Klaus. "The Black Body and the Jewish Body: A Comparison of Medical Images." *Patterns of Prejudice* 36 (2002): 17-34.

8. Hödl, Klaus. "Medizinischer Antisemitismus oder Antisemitismus in der Medizin? Historische Wurzeln und Charakterisierungsversuche eines Phänomens." In *Antisemitismusforschung in den Wissenschaften*, ed. Werner Bergmann and Mona Körte, 161-185. Berlin: Metropol, 2004.

9. Hödl, Klaus. "Der "jüdische Körper" in seiner Differenz. Textuelle und performative Konstruktionen." In *Marginalisierte Körper. Beiträge zur Soziologie und Geschichte des anderen Körpers*, ed. Torsten Junge and Imke Schmincke, 63-77. Münster: Unrast, 2007.

10. Knorr-Cetina, Karin. *Die Fabrikation von Erkentniss: Zur Anthropologie der Naturwissenschaft.* Frankfurt am Main: Suhrkamp, 1984.

11. Latour, Bruno and Steve Woolgar. *Laboratory Life: The Construction of Scientific Facts.* Princeton: Princeton University Press, 1986.

12. Lerner, Paul F. *Hysterical Men: War, Psychiatry and the Politics of Trauma in Germany, 1890-1930.* Ithaca: Cornell University Press, 2003.

13. Lerner, Paul F. "Circulation and Representation: Jews, Department Stores and Cosmopolitan Consumption in Germany, ca. 1880s-1930s." *European Review of History* 17 (2010) (forthcoming)

14. Muller, Jerry Z. *Capitalism and the Jews.* Princeton: Princeton

University Press, 2010.

15. Oxaal, Ivar and Walter R. Weitzmann. "The Jews of Pre-1914 Vienna: An Exploration of Basic Sociological Dimensions." *Leo Baeck Institute Yearbook* 30 (1985): 395-432.

16. Penslar, Derek J.. *Shylock's Children: Economics and Jewish Identity in Modern Europe.* Berkeley: University of California Press, 2001.

17. Plaggenborg, Stefan. *Revolutionskultur: Menschenbilder und kulturelle Praxis in Sowjetrussland zwischen Oktoberrevolution und Stalinismus.* Cologne: Böhlau, 1996.

18. Starks, Tricia. *The Body Soviet: Propaganda, Hygiene, and the Revolutionary State.* Madison: University of Wisconsin Press, 2008.

19. Volkov, Shulamit. "Antisemitism as a Cultural Code: Reflections on the History and Historiography of Antisemitism in Imperial Germany." *Leo Baeck Institute Yearbook* 23 (1978): 25-46.

20. Volkov, Shulamit. "The Written Matter and the Spoken Word: On the Gap Between Pre-1914 and Nazi Anti-Semitism." In *Unanswered Questions: Nazi Germany and the Genocide of the Jews*, ed. François Furet, 33-53. New York: Schocken Books, 1989.

21. Wildmann, Daniel. *Der veränderbare Körper. Jüdische Turner, Männlichkeit und das Wiedergewinnen von Geschichte in Deutschland um 1900.* Tübingen: Mohr Siebeck, 2009.